Afghanistan A
the Drawdown

COUNCIL *on*
FOREIGN
RELATIONS

Center for Preventive Action

Council Special Report No. 67
November 2013

Seth G. Jones and Keith Crane

Afghanistan After the Drawdown

Contents

Foreword

The United States has now been at war in Afghanistan for more than a decade. The sacrifice in blood and treasure has been substantial. Some 2,300 American servicemen and women have lost their lives, more than 19,000 have been injured, and nearly $650 billion has been spent over the course of the United States' longest war. The results, however, can only be described as inconclusive. The reach and effectiveness of the Afghan central government remain circumscribed, challenged by various armed groups and undermined by pervasive corruption. The economy has grown rapidly, albeit from a low starting place, but remains largely dependent on international aid flows that will certainly shrink.

The combination of high costs and middling returns has left the American public increasingly skeptical of the utility of the U.S. commitment to Afghanistan. The 2011 death of Osama bin Laden, mastermind of the 9/11 attacks that brought the American military to Afghanistan in 2001, only reinforced that perception. Yet the United States retains interests in Afghanistan, including preventing the reemergence of a terrorist safe haven and promoting stability in the region, which could be further undermined by a total withdrawal of American military forces.

As this Council Special Report explains, 2014 will be a pivotal year for Afghanistan. An election will, presumably, bring a new president to Kabul. The U.S. military will complete its transfer of responsibility to the Afghan National Security Forces, making the war effort Afghan-led. And, as donor financing begins to come down, the Afghan economy will need to find sustainable, internal sources of growth.

Authors Seth G. Jones and Keith Crane recommend a number of steps the United States can and should take to advance its interests during this transition. During the presidential elections, they write, Washington should encourage multiethnic political coalitions to increase the representativeness of (and decrease divisions within) the Afghan government. The United States should also help the Afghan

National Security Forces and other relevant authorities secure election sites and improve the quality and transparency of the election itself. They further recommend a continued military presence in Afghanistan of eight thousand to twelve thousand U.S. soldiers pursuing a "foreign internal defense mission." These troops, ideally with further support from NATO and other allies, would conduct strikes against terrorists and train, advise, and assist Afghan national and local forces; as is obvious, all this depends on the willingness of the Afghan government to agree. The authors also encourage the United States and other donors to continue their civilian aid pledges, provided that Afghanistan meets its commitments to good governance and transparency, and suggest small-scale economic initiatives to help improve relationships among countries in the region. Finally, they acknowledge that there is unlikely to be a major change in the troubled U.S.-Pakistan relationship, in no small part because Islamabad continues to provide a sanctuary to the Afghan Taliban. As a result, the authors recommend that Washington seeks ways to reduce its dependence on Islamabad for what the United States does in Afghanistan and tightly calibrates its military assistance to the Pakistani government.

Afghanistan After the Drawdown is a sober, thoughtful assessment of Afghanistan's prospects in the coming year and beyond. It offers U.S. policymakers a realistic set of options in the political, security, and economic realms that are consistent with the scope of American interests, the resources the United States can reasonably bring to bear, and Afghan realities. Despite the many challenges facing Afghanistan in the years ahead, this report argues persuasively that the United States still can, and should, seek a role in its future.

Richard N. Haass
President
Council on Foreign Relations
November 2013

Acknowledgments

We would like to thank CFR President Richard N. Haass and Director of Studies James M. Lindsay for their support of this project. We owe a special debt of gratitude to members of our advisory committee, in particular Ambassador Marc Grossman, who provided several sets of comments over the course of the project. Peter Ackerman, General John Allen, Steven D. Biddle, John A. Gastright, Frederick W. Kagan, Clare Lockhart, Steve Mann, Daniel S. Markey, Paul D. Miller, Ronald E. Neumann, David E. Sanger, Ashley J. Tellis, Andrew Wilder, and Micah Zenko provided helpful critiques, which greatly improved the quality of the report.

We are also deeply grateful to those U.S. officials from the White House, State Department, Defense Department, U.S. Agency for International Development, and intelligence community who took time out of their busy schedules to speak with us—including on trips to Afghanistan in September and October 2013. Outside of the U.S. government, we thank the government officials, academics, and other civilians from Afghanistan, Pakistan, India, Russia, and NATO countries for their thoughtful comments and willingness to discuss Afghanistan after the U.S. drawdown.

The highly professional staff of CFR's Washington and New York offices was a pleasure to work with. In particular, we would like to thank Patricia Dorff and her Publications team, as well as Anna Feuer, for their valuable assistance. Lastly, we would like to thank Paul B. Stares for shepherding this project from inception to conclusion. He played an extraordinary role in structuring the project, drafting members of the Advisory Committee, organizing and leading meetings of the Committee, and steering the paper through the publications process.

This publication was made possible by a grant from Carnegie Corporation of New York. The statements made and views expressed are solely our own.

Seth G. Jones and Keith Crane

Council Special Report

Introduction

Afghanistan will undergo three major transitions in 2014: from a Hamid Karzai–led government to one presumably headed by another president following the 2014 election; from a U.S.-led to an Afghan-led counterinsurgency; and from an economy driven by foreign expenditures on military support and assistance to one more reliant on domestic sources of growth, as the United States and other countries reduce their presence. The United States and its allies will need to shape each of these transitions in ways that safeguard their interests.

Even after most U.S. forces are withdrawn by the end of 2014, the United States will continue to have important national interests in Afghanistan and South Asia. First, al-Qaeda's global leadership is still located along the Afghanistan-Pakistan border, though it has been weakened by persistent U.S. strikes. A civil war or successful Taliban-led insurgency would likely allow al-Qaeda and other terrorist groups such as the Tehrik-e-Taliban Pakistan, Haqqani network, and Lashkar-e-Taiba to increase their presence in Afghanistan. Most of these groups have already expanded their presence in Afghanistan over the past several years and have conducted attacks either against the U.S. homeland (al-Qaeda and Tehrik-e-Taliban Pakistan), U.S. forces and U.S. government installations in Afghanistan (Taliban and Haqqani network), or U.S. citizens in the region (Lashkar-e-Taiba and al-Qaeda).

Second, a burgeoning war could increase regional instability as India, Pakistan, Iran, and Russia support a mix of Afghan central government forces, substate militias, and insurgent groups. Pakistan, in particular, would likely experience increasing violence and refugee flows if the war in Afghanistan spills over its border, as it did in the 1980s and 1990s. Growing conflict and radicalization in Pakistan, in turn, raise concerns about the security of its nuclear stockpile.[1]

Finally, a U.S. military departure from Afghanistan—if it were to happen—could foster a perception, however misplaced, that the United

States is not a reliable ally. Al-Qaeda and associated movements would likely view a withdrawal of U.S. military forces as their most important victory since the departure of Soviet forces from Afghanistan in 1989.

Although the United States retains significant interests in Afghanistan, many U.S. politicians and a majority of the public wish to see an end to U.S. participation in the conflict after more than a decade of war. Following 9/11, there was substantial support for U.S. military operations in Afghanistan to overthrow the Taliban regime, which harbored Osama bin Laden and other al-Qaeda leaders. According to an October 2001 public opinion poll, 90 percent of Americans—including 97 percent of Republicans and 85 percent of Democrats—supported U.S. military action in Afghanistan.[2] After the overthrow of the Taliban regime, however, U.S. goals expanded to include defeating al-Qaeda and its associates and building a stable, economically prosperous, and democratic state. Over the next decade, U.S. public support for some of these broader goals began to decline as U.S. casualties escalated, Taliban attacks increased, and evidence of massive corruption among senior Afghan government officials mounted. A July 2013 poll conducted by the *Washington Post* and ABC News found that only 28 percent of Americans believe the war in Afghanistan was worth fighting.[3]

As President Barack Obama and other U.S. officials outlined in early 2013 and at various international conferences, U.S. policy in Afghanistan has two primary objectives: targeting the remnants of al-Qaeda and other affiliates so that they cannot launch attacks against the U.S. homeland; and training, assisting, and advising Afghan forces so that Afghanistan can provide for its own security.[4] To accomplish these objectives, U.S. policy has focused on strengthening Afghan National Security Forces (ANSF); building a stronger political and security partnership with Afghanistan; supporting an Afghan peace process; enhancing regional cooperation; and fostering economic growth in Afghanistan.[5]

These objectives are still important. The United States should continue to target terrorist groups that threaten the United States and help the Afghan government provide for its own security. While some administration officials insist these objectives have largely been met, this conclusion is premature.[6] Though weakened, al-Qaeda has survived U.S. counterterrorism operations. Perhaps more troubling, there appears to be a slight increase in the number of terrorist groups operating in Afghanistan compared to a decade ago, according to U.S. military and intelligence officials in Afghanistan.[7]

To accomplish its primary objectives, the United States should take the following policy steps:

- *Promote multiethnic coalitions—rather than individual candidates—for the 2014 presidential election and, for the eventual winner, encourage the appointment of a cabinet and senior officials that represent Afghanistan's ethnic and cultural constituencies.* Over the long run, stability will hinge on the ability of Afghanistan's main Pashtun, Uzbek, Tajik, Hazara, and other constituencies to reach a political consensus during and after the election. In addition, the United States should provide financial and other support to improve poll-worker screening, expand observer missions at voting centers, and move the vote-counting process from voting centers to provincial offices before and during the 2014 presidential election.

- *Pursue a foreign internal defense mission that includes between eight thousand and twelve thousand residual American troops, plus additional NATO forces.* Their goal should be to target al-Qaeda and its allies, as well as to train, advise, and assist Afghan forces. The United States should encourage the Afghan government to sign the bilateral security agreement as soon as possible. But in the meantime, U.S. policymakers should still indicate their willingness to provide an enduring military presence in Afghanistan after 2014.

- *Support Afghan government–led discussions with the Taliban and other groups over prisoner exchanges, local cease-fires, and the reintegration of fighters.* Taliban leaders have been—and will likely continue to be—willing to negotiate over this limited set of issues. But U.S. policymakers should recognize that a comprehensive peace settlement with the Taliban is unlikely in the foreseeable future. Most insurgencies end with one side winning on the battlefield, not at the negotiating table. In addition, Taliban leaders have few incentives to conclude a peace settlement today, in part because they believe their prospects for military victory will improve after the U.S. drawdown.

- *Work with the United Kingdom, the European Union, Japan, Germany, and other donors to sustain funding levels for public services like education and public health care through 2017 and beyond.* Foreign donors should continue to provide $5 billion a year in funding to sustain the ANSF. The United States and other international donors should also provide economic assistance of $3.3 billion to $3.9 billion a year through 2017, as recommended by the World Bank at the Tokyo

Conference—if Afghanistan's government adheres to its commitments under the Tokyo Agreement.

- *Support regional economic initiatives to improve the regional business climate.* U.S. diplomats should encourage "economic détente" between Pakistan and India, working with Pakistan to follow through on its 2011 decision to grant India most-favored-nation trading status.

If these recommendations are implemented, Afghanistan will likely be able to contain the insurgency, ensure the Afghan government is not overthrown, and prevent the reemergence of al-Qaeda and its allies post-2014—all vital U.S. interests. Afghanistan may also be able to sustain the improvement in incomes, democratic freedom, health, and educational levels it has enjoyed since the fall of the Taliban.[8] The United States and other foreign donors have provided the security and funds that have contributed to these improvements. However, U.S. support should not be open-ended; it should be conditions-based. Continuing U.S. support is possible at a reasonable cost to the United States and Afghanistan's other foreign donors, so long as Afghan leaders hold the presidential election in 2014, continue to enhance the capabilities of the ANSF, take steps to improve governance, and reach a bilateral security agreement with Washington. The United States should also continue to assess the state of al-Qaeda and associated terrorist groups. If al-Qaeda were to lose its sanctuary in Afghanistan and Pakistan, and become unable or unwilling to strike the United States, there would be little strategic rationale to keep U.S. military forces in Afghanistan.

Over the past decade, there has been progress in Afghanistan. Afghan forces have taken over most of the fighting from U.S. and other foreign forces. Total U.S. expenditures for U.S. involvement in Afghanistan laid out in this report would be less than a sixth of Fiscal Year 2011 levels of roughly $100 billion per year. In light of the likely benefits provided by such an effort, this level of funding should be affordable even during this period of U.S. government budget stringency. But a U.S. failure to implement these recommendations—particularly a U.S. decision to leave Afghanistan—would increase the likelihood of an al-Qaeda resurgence, regional instability, and a deterioration of human (including women's) rights. It is a lesson the United States should have learned over two decades ago when it cut off aid to Afghanistan after the Soviet withdrawal—an era followed by the rise of the Taliban and its al-Qaeda allies.

Afghanistan's Transitions: 2014 and Beyond

U.S. policymakers face a complex set of challenges that stem from the political, security, and economic transitions under way in Afghanistan. These challenges are interrelated. To complicate matters, these transitions are also heavily affected by Afghanistan's relations with its neighbors. Regional dynamics will have to be managed effectively to ensure a successful drawdown of the United States' commitment beyond 2014.

THE POLITICAL TRANSITION

The presidential election, which is tentatively scheduled for April 2014, is perhaps the most important political event in 2014 for Afghans.[9] It will be marred by violence and corruption. The election could lead to deterioration in the security environment if competing groups dispute the outcome. Substate actors, especially power brokers from northern and western Afghanistan, may lose faith in the central government and accelerate efforts to rearm. These fissures could undermine the cohesiveness of the Afghan National Army and other security agencies and affect the scope and degree of support from neighboring states.

Politics in Afghanistan exist within a milieu of blocs. At the national level, the most powerful political bloc is based on President Hamid Karzai's patronage network. It extends from the presidential palace in Kabul to Afghanistan's ministries; provincial, district, and justice officials; businesses; tribes (including the president's Popalzai tribe); and other actors.[10] A number of presidential hopefuls will try to leverage his patronage network. President Karzai's political opponents recently formed two loose coalitions. The Afghan National Front (ANF) was announced in mid-November 2012 and is led by such figures as Ahmad Zia Massood, Mohammad Mohaqqeq, and Abdul Rashid Dostum. In late 2012, Abdullah Abdullah established the National Coalition of Afghanistan (NCA). Both coalitions have similar goals: institute a parliamentary system to distribute power away from the executive branch, devolve more authority from Kabul to the provinces, and insist on the participation of Afghanistan's non-Pashtun groups in peace negotiations.

An even more complex set of political networks has developed at the regional and local levels. The regional blocs include Hezb-e-Islami Afghanistan, Jamiat-e-Islami, Hezb-e Wahdat-e Islami, and Junbesh-e Milli, among others. These organizations have lost power and relevance over the past decade, but could become more important if the Taliban makes gains on the battlefield and the central government begins to fracture.

If the 2014 election is broadly accepted, the likelihood for stability in Afghanistan will improve. The size, mission, and duration of the U.S. force in Afghanistan after 2014 will also play a major role in determining the political stability of Afghanistan. If Afghans perceive the size of the force as too small or short-term, influential leaders are likely to be alarmed, encouraging them to bolster their militias to compensate for the diminished U.S. presence.

THE SECURITY TRANSITION

U.S. policymakers will face several security challenges during—and after—the transition. By the end of 2014, the NATO-led mission in Afghanistan will shift from Operation Enduring Freedom, which has included a range of combat and reconstruction tasks, to Operation Resolute Support, which will focus on training and advising Afghan forces.

During and after this transition, insurgents will likely gain some ground as the U.S. and other foreign militaries reduce their presence. The insurgency will remain diverse and include a range of groups led by the Taliban, Haqqani network, allied Pashtun tribes and clans, drug trafficking organizations, and local militia forces supported by neighboring states like Pakistan and Iran.

Terrorist groups, including al-Qaeda, will presumably attempt to increase their presence in Afghanistan. Al-Qaeda leaders likely believe the U.S. drawdown will allow them more freedom of movement in provinces such as Kunar and Nuristan. Al-Qaeda's paramilitary commander and emir for northeastern Afghanistan, Faruq al-Qatari, is already attempting to expand al-Qaeda's footprint in the northeast.[11] Since al-Qaeda currently lacks the legitimacy and power to establish a sanctuary in Afghanistan and Pakistan on its own, it has attempted to leverage the capabilities of local militant networks like the Haqqani network. This symbiotic arrangement provides al-Qaeda some operational flexibility to access existing resources.

If competing groups dispute the outcome of the 2014 presidential election, substate actors, especially influential power brokers from the north and west, may lose faith in the central government and accelerate efforts to rearm. Furthermore, a failure by the United States and Afghanistan to sign a bilateral security agreement would likely fracture the ANSF along ethnic and social cleavages if the United States withdraws all of its military forces. Finally, the overall quality of the ANSF and the Afghan Local Police will affect the success of the insurgency and the ability of terrorist groups to reestablish safe havens in Afghanistan.

Afghan security forces, especially the Afghan National Army, have shown improvement in their ability to fight despite incurring in 2013 the highest numbers of casualties of the war to date. In Kandahar, Provincial Chief of Police Abdul Raziq and Afghan forces—the ANSF, Afghan Local Police, and National Directorate of Security units—have held territory in several districts that are strategically important for the Taliban, such as Arghandab. In June 2013, Afghan national and local forces successfully conducted a major clearing operation along the Kunar-Nuristan border with some U.S. air support. Despite this overall progress, the ANSF also has notable deficiencies in such areas as intelligence collection and logistics, which have hurt their battlefield performance. In some provinces, such as Helmand, the ANSF has been unable to retain control of some areas seized by U.S. Marine Corps forces over the past four years. In other provinces, such as Khowst and Paktika, insurgents from the Haqqani network increased territorial control in 2013 after the withdrawal of U.S. and Afghan forces from several bases. Afghan forces have also been unable to prevent several high-profile attacks, such as on the U.S. Consulate in Herat in September 2013 and the Ariana Hotel in Kabul in June 2013. The weakness of some Afghan forces poses a challenge to the success of the security transition and, as noted in the recommendations, should be adequately addressed by U.S. military trainers.

THE ECONOMIC TRANSITION

The primary economic tasks facing U.S. policymakers are to help foster economic growth and to ensure adequate funding for the ANSF and public services. Since 2001, Afghanistan's GDP has grown an average of roughly 11 percent annually.[12] Four factors have driven this growth. First, despite the insurgency, levels of violence in much of the country are down compared to those during the civil war of the 1990s. Afghans have responded to improved security by investing in housing, small businesses, and farms. Second, the international presence in Afghanistan has stimulated the Afghan economy through purchases of goods and services. Third, foreign donors have paid for a rapid expansion of public services, especially education and health care, and made substantial investments in roads, schools, clinics, and irrigation systems. The World Bank estimates that combined international spending on security assistance and civilian aid in 2011 was equivalent to 100 percent of GDP. Civilian aid alone ($6 billion) equaled 40 percent of GDP.[13] Fourth, investments in transportation and communications have contributed to productivity gains and growth in those services.

Despite these changes, most Afghans still rely on agriculture, licit and illicit, as their primary source of income. About 70 percent of Afghanistan's population works in subsistence agriculture, even though agriculture generates only one-third of GDP. Opium is the most important cash crop.

Following the drawdown, Afghanistan is likely to become poorer and more agrarian. In 2014 and 2015, GDP may fall because of the decline in demand for Afghan services as the number of troops decreases; reductions in public services due to cuts in foreign budgetary support and limited access by assistance providers to violent areas; and cuts in public investment resulting from reduced foreign assistance. All of these factors will reduce incomes in Afghanistan. Afghanistan's expenditures on security forces and public services will continue to depend on foreign funding, of which the United States is likely to remain the largest provider. Donors have promised continued support, especially to cover the costs of Afghanistan's army and police. But problems with corruption and war weariness are already resulting in reductions in aid, including from the United States. Moreover, the Afghan government has not met its obligations in the Tokyo Mutual Accountability Framework, where it pledged to undertake reforms in areas such as women's rights to ensure continued international economic support.[14]

THE REGIONAL DIMENSION

Afghanistan has long been entangled in a "Great Game" among neighboring states and global powers.[15] Several factors will likely determine the shape and influence of regional dynamics on the three transitions. A U.S. decision to withdraw all of its remaining military forces from the region by 2015 would intensify security competition among regional powers. Outside powers would almost certainly back various substate actors, exacerbating ethnic and other fissures in Afghanistan. In particular, the rivalry between India and Pakistan is already intensifying in Afghanistan. Indian officials have expressed alarm that Afghanistan will become a base for anti-Indian terrorist groups if the Taliban makes advances on the battlefield. In response, India has likely increased its support to Uzbek, Tajik, and even Pashtun power brokers in Afghanistan—as well as to members of the Karzai government. Pakistan, for its part, will likely continue to support both the Taliban insurgency and peace negotiations, with an eye toward assessing which track is likely to succeed.

As Table 1 shows, most of Afghanistan's neighbors generally prefer a stable central government, but one that protects their interests. Russia, China, Iran, Pakistan, and India all signed the "Heart of Asia" Istanbul declaration in November 2011, which mandated specific follow-on actions in such areas as counterterrorism, counternarcotics, trade, and investment.[16]

A second factor is the state of the insurgency. An ascendant Taliban and a weakened Afghan central government would cause Afghanistan's neighbors to support a range of competing substate actors as Afghanistan fell back into a civil war.[17] If the Taliban were to gain momentum, the most significant source of friction would likely be between India and Pakistan, though other neighbors would probably back their traditional allies.

TABLE 1: REGIONAL DYNAMICS

Country	State Interests	Future Position If Afghan Government Remains in Relative Control	If Taliban Gains Momentum
India	Support Indian-allied government in Kabul; minimize Islamabad's influence; weaken anti-Indian terrorist groups	Provide economic and nonlethal aid to Kabul, but also maintain ties to anti-Taliban leaders (especially in the north)	Would likely increase funding, training, and lethal assistance to anti-Taliban leaders
Pakistan	Establish Pakistan-allied government in Kabul; minimize New Delhi's influence; prevent anti-Pakistan groups from gaining a foothold; foster trade	Retain Taliban safe havens in Pakistan; support Taliban and other insurgents, as well as peace negotiations	Could increase support to the Taliban and other insurgents; might also reach out to northern groups
Iran	Assist allies in Afghanistan's government and substate groups near the Iranian border; prevent permanent U.S. bases in Afghanistan; foster trade	Support both central government and regional allies	Might support anti-Taliban forces to prevent a Taliban takeover; might also maintain limited ties to the Taliban and other insurgent groups
Russia	Encourage stable central government that tries to curb the flow of terrorists and narcotics into Central Asia and Russia	Provide limited assistance to the central government, but maintain ties to power brokers in northern Afghanistan	Would likely increase support—intelligence, money, and lethal aid—to anti-Taliban forces in the north
China	Support stable government that protects Chinese interests and curbs activities of Uighur militants and East Turkestan Islamic Party	Expand ties to Kabul, but also maintain contacts with Taliban to ensure access to mines and other investments	Could support Pakistan, but would likely be concerned about spread of terrorism
Tajikistan	Encourage stable government that includes representatives from northern groups and stabilizes border region	Provide political support to northern power brokers, especially Tajiks	Would consider increasing aid to northern groups
Uzbekistan	Support stable government that cracks down on terrorist groups and includes representatives from northern groups	Provide financial support to northern power brokers, especially Uzbeks	Would consider increasing aid to northern groups to prevent the Islamic Movement of Uzbekistan and other groups from gaining a foothold

Policy Choices

In light of the three transitions Afghanistan faces, U.S. policymakers need to make choices that will affect the country's political, security, and economic future. U.S. officials also face important choices in dealing with Afghanistan's complex regional environment.

PRESIDENTIAL ELECTION

U.S. policymakers have several options regarding the 2014 presidential election. First, the U.S. government can adopt a hands-off approach that leaves the election process to the Afghan government and international organizations like the United Nations Assistance Mission in Afghanistan (UNAMA). Some Afghans have worried that a hands-on U.S. approach could be interpreted as foreign meddling and undermine the credibility of the election.[18] But outside countries, including the United States, have played crucial roles in facilitating numerous political transitions and supporting democratization efforts across the globe, including during previous elections in Afghanistan.[19] A hands-off approach could also increase the likelihood that Pakistan, India, Russia, and Iran would influence the election based on their interests. Left unchecked, for instance, Iranian support in the election—including of specific candidates—would likely undermine U.S. interests.

A second option would entail the private, and perhaps public, involvement of U.S. diplomats in the technical aspects of ensuring a free-and-fair election.[20] The United States could assist in specific areas where there are concerns about fraud or neglect, such as in response to allegations of ballot stuffing. This might include identifying instances where fraud has occurred (or could occur), bringing it to the attention of Afghan and international officials, and working to fix any improprieties. Much of the international donor community cares greatly about process. Though laudable, it would be important not to set unrealistic goals for a free-and-fair process in a country with an ongoing civil war, a culture of patronage, and some of the highest corruption rates in the world.[21] There will almost certainly be corruption in the election; the challenge will be to minimize it.

A third option would involve U.S. diplomats encouraging the candidates to recruit a team—and, for the eventual winner, ultimately appointing a cabinet—that reflects Afghanistan's ethnic, religious, and other constituencies. This would involve White House, State Department, and Defense Department officials developing a communications strategy—complete with talking points—that reinforces the importance of multiethnic coalitions in meetings with their Afghan counterparts. U.S. officials would need to communicate this message at several stages: during the campaign; while the votes are counted; after the announcements of preliminary and final results; and after the inauguration of a new president. But there are risks with such a hands-on approach, since some Afghans might accuse the United States of foreign meddling.

A fourth option would be to champion a specific candidate for president. U.S. officials could publicly support a candidate by making favorable statements, as well as by privately offering funding or other resources. But this option could fail to produce the desired outcome and would likely taint the legitimacy of the winner.

PEACE TALKS

Peace negotiations will continue to be an important component of the political and security transitions in Afghanistan. In past insurgencies, the likelihood of a peace settlement has depended on the type and extent of external support that combatants received; the length, duration, and status of the war; and the existence and role of a third-party mediator to help with peace negotiations.[22] Drawing on these lessons, U.S. policymakers have three broad options as they weigh peace discussions.

One is for the United States—especially the White House and State Department—to play a leading role in negotiating a comprehensive peace settlement with the Taliban.[23] The United States might take the lead in peace talks because the Taliban has thus far refused to negotiate directly with the Karzai government. Some proponents of U.S.-led peace discussions contend that negotiations are desirable even if they fail.[24] They argue that insurgencies often end with a political settlement, not on the battlefield. But U.S.-led discussions face several challenges. The United States would be serving as both a mediator and a combatant; it would not be a neutral party. More important, although negotiations can be useful, many insurgencies end with a military victory by one side or the other, rather than a peace settlement. Since 1955, of the roughly fifty-five civil wars in which adversaries have fought for control of the central government, 75 percent ended with a clear victory.[25] In addition, wars ended by military victory (rather than through peace settlements) are more likely to stay ended.[26] This may well be true for Afghanistan.

Alternatively, the United States could play a supporting role in the negotiations, rather than a leading one, leaving leadership to the Afghan government and the Taliban.[27] U.S. diplomats might refrain from participating in meetings between Taliban and Afghan government representatives until they reach a more advanced stage of discussions. Under one variant of this option, a third party, such as a senior diplomat from a Gulf state or a UN representative, might act as a mediator or facilitator.[28] A third-party mediator could be useful with—or without—direct U.S. involvement in peace talks. The risk with a supporting U.S. role, however, is that the United States could lose some leverage in influencing the negotiations.

A final option is to abandon peace negotiations, at least for the moment, and focus on other policy steps, such as improving ANSF capabilities, holding the 2014 presidential election, and supporting regional economic initiatives. But this approach undercuts the possibility, however slim, of a peaceful end to three and a half decades of fighting. Many Afghans are tired of war, so peace talks may be worth a shot.

THE U.S. MILITARY PRESENCE

The size, composition, and duration of a continued U.S. military presence in Afghanistan are the most frequently discussed components of the transition. As shown in Table 2, the financial costs of deploying U.S. troops in Afghanistan have been high.

Budgetary pressures to reduce these costs have been an important factor in the current drawdown. As the United States reduces its presence, there are four plausible military options for 2015 and beyond.[29]

TABLE 2: U.S. COSTS OF THE AFGHANISTAN WAR (IN BILLIONS OF DOLLARS)

	FY2004	FY2005	FY2006	FY2007	FY2008	FY2009	FY2010	FY2011	FY2012 Request
War Funding	14.6	20.0	19.0	39.2	43.4	59.5	93.8	118.6	113.7
State/USAID	2.2	2.8	1.1	1.9	2.7	3.1	5.7	4.1	4.3

Source: Amy Belasco, "The Cost of Iraq, Afghanistan, and Other Global War on Terror Operations Since 9/11," Congressional Research Service, March 29, 2011, p. 17.

The first, often referred to as the "zero option," is to withdraw all U.S. forces from Afghanistan.[30] This option assumes that the United States has no major strategic interests left in Afghanistan or that a military presence would not achieve U.S. objectives at an acceptable cost.[31] It could also occur with a failure by U.S. and Afghan officials to conclude a bilateral security agreement. According to this view, al-Qaeda's leadership has already been severely weakened because of the relentless U.S. counterterrorism campaign and hence U.S. forces are no longer needed in Afghanistan to combat a diminished threat.[32]

The second option involves reducing the U.S. military footprint to between one thousand and three thousand personnel in Afghanistan, configured solely for counterterrorism operations.[33] The U.S. military would work with the CIA, other U.S. intelligence agencies, and Afghan units to kill or capture terrorists affiliated with al-Qaeda and associated groups to prevent their resurgence in Afghanistan. There are several possible U.S. force packages for this mission. One might include a squadron of "Tier 1" or other special operations task force units, drawn from units attached to Joint Special Operations Command. These forces would operate with a small number of NATO special operations forces and work closely with Afghan special operations units, such as the Ktah Khas, to conduct operations. This option would also include limited "enablers," such as unmanned aerial vehicles and intelligence, surveillance, and reconnaissance assets.

The zero and counterterrorism options would significantly reduce (or eliminate, in the former case) the financial burden on the United States of supporting U.S. forces in Afghanistan, and minimize (or eliminate) American combat deaths. But both options pose substantial risks. U.S. forces would have little or no mandate and limited or no capabilities after 2015 to assist the Afghan government if the Taliban threatened to overrun a major city or even topple the government. It would also increase the probability that Afghanistan would be used as a beachhead for al-Qaeda and other militant groups.[34] Iraq after the U.S. withdrawal is illustrative: al-Qaeda in Iraq has regrouped since 2011. It conducts attacks at a high tempo and was instrumental in establishing an affiliate, Jabhat al-Nusra, in Syria.

Third is a light foreign internal defense option, which would include between four thousand and six thousand U.S. forces, plus additional NATO forces. It would expand the U.S. mission from counterterrorism to foreign internal defense.[35] A small number of U.S. special operations forces would train, advise, and assist the Afghan National Army, Afghan National Police, and Afghan Local Police.[36] U.S. forces might also be required to help Afghan forces provide security for the 2014 election and backup protection for U.S. diplomats. This option would involve keeping more U.S. forces in Afghanistan than the counterterrorism option, along with a small contingent of NATO forces, to ensure the Afghan government is not overthrown and to help Afghan forces degrade the insurgency. The foreign internal defense mission would rely on U.S. special operations and other forces to help the Afghans conduct counterterrorism and counterinsurgency operations, as U.S. Army Green Berets have done in the Philippines, Colombia, and other campaigns.

Fourth is a larger foreign internal defense option that would consist of between eight thousand and twelve thousand U.S. forces. This option would include a larger force package of U.S. Army Special Forces, unmanned aerial vehicles, a conventional security force assistance team, attack aircraft, and other enablers. A larger force package would allow the United States to deploy more trainers and advisers to a greater number of areas, facilitating Afghan counterinsurgency operations.

The light and heavy foreign internal defense options would involve higher financial costs than the first and second options, albeit still at much lower levels than today. They also risk a higher number of U.S. casualties, though U.S. forces would concentrate primarily on training Afghans, not fighting. At the same time, both options allow the United States to continue to improve the combat capability of Afghanistan's national and local security forces, as well as respond *in extremis* to situations such as a Taliban advance on a major city or the potential overthrow of the Afghan government. The United States could reduce its force numbers as Afghan capabilities improve. Table 3 summarizes the four options and their likely budgetary costs.

ECONOMIC GROWTH

There are several policy options for fostering economic growth during the transition. The United States and other donors could concentrate assistance efforts on supporting rural assistance programs. Substantial gains in agricultural output are possible if irrigation systems are expanded, incentives and systems to ensure efficient use of water and maintenance of irrigation systems are improved, and further

TABLE 3: OVERVIEW OF MILITARY OPERATIONS[37]

Option	Primary Mission	Troop Strength (U.S. forces)	Annual Cost (in billions of 2012 U.S. dollars)
Zero Option	No military mission, but could include civilian, diplomatic, and intelligence missions	0	$0
Counterterrorism	Conduct counterterrorism strikes against al-Qaeda and associated groups with Afghan partners	1,000–3,000	$0.6–$1.8
Light Foreign Internal Defense	Conduct counterterrorism strikes; limited train, advise, and assist to Afghan units	4,000–6,000	$2.4–$3.5
Heavy Foreign Internal Defense	Conduct counterterrorism strikes; more robust train, advise, and assist to Afghan units	8,000–12,000	$4.7–$7.1

Source: Author calculations based on average cost per service member from Amy Belasco, "The Cost of Iraq, Afghanistan, and Other Global War on Terror Operations Since 9/11," Congressional Research Service, March 29, 2011, p. 23.

investments are made to expand and maintain roads and market access for agricultural inputs and products.

Another option is to channel assistance toward developing mining or the oil and gas industries in hopes of generating substantial revenues that can be tapped by the Afghan government. Afghanistan has potentially commercially exploitable deposits of iron ore, copper, natural gas, and other metals and minerals.[38] However, the World Bank notes the need for substantial investment—between $6 billion and $15 billion—to open these mines. Extracting these metals or oil and gas will be expensive and challenging. Because of infrastructure costs, institutional weaknesses, and the poor investment climate in Afghanistan, mining or oil and gas extraction are unlikely to make major contributions to the Afghan economy in the near to medium term.

Finally, the United States and other donors could invest in improving transnational transportation networks across Afghanistan. Increased cross-border transit, especially between India and Afghanistan, could strengthen economic ties among Afghanistan, Pakistan, and India, potentially resulting in a decline in tensions between Pakistan and the other two countries. Increasing transit to Central Asia is less promising. Volumes of trade among Central Asia, Pakistan, and India are low and likely to remain so. Afghanistan's rough terrain, the poor state of its highways, levels of insecurity, and bribes demanded from transit companies are not conducive to transit traffic between these two areas. Until security improves and costs fall, Afghanistan is unlikely to become a major international corridor.

REGIONAL DYNAMICS

There are several U.S. policy options for dealing with Afghanistan's complex regional environment, especially with Pakistan and India. The first is to more aggressively encourage Pakistan and India to pursue détente, especially economic détente. "We will pick up the threads from where we left in 1999," Pakistan prime minister Nawaz Sharif said after his 2013 election victory, referring to his previous stint as prime minister. "That is the roadmap that I have for improvement of relations between Pakistan and India."[39] As prime minister in the late 1990s, Sharif signed a number of agreements with his Indian counterpart, Atal Bihari Vajpayee, including the Lahore Declaration. Under the Lahore

Declaration, both sides agreed to intensify their efforts to resolve the Kashmir dispute and reduce the risk of accidental or unauthorized use of nuclear weapons. But India has been reluctant to support a more active U.S. role in helping negotiate détente with Pakistan. Assuming Sharif is serious about détente, there is still opposition among some Pakistan military officials to closer relations with India.

A second option is for U.S. policymakers to develop a more aggressive policy toward Pakistan to root out militant groups. Examples might include tying U.S. military assistance to Pakistan's progress in countering military groups or continuing to shift U.S. supply routes from Pakistan to the northern route through Central Asia. On the latter issue, insurgents extort payments from trucking companies, especially those hauling cargo for NATO forces. Rerouting supply routes, even at an additional cost, would cut into revenues insurgents have relied upon to prosecute the war.

The challenge for U.S. policymakers is that Pakistan's military, through its Inter-Services Intelligence (ISI) directorate, continues to provide some support to the Taliban and other insurgents. It does so to counterbalance India in Afghanistan and in the hopes of encouraging an Afghan government allied with Pakistan. In the past, those insurgencies that have received support from external states triumphed more than 50 percent of the time, while those with no support won only 17 percent of the time. Sanctuary is almost as important. Insurgents have been successful approximately 43 percent of the time when they enjoyed sanctuary.[40] Consequently, depriving the Taliban of external support or sanctuary would decrease its odds of overthrowing the Afghan government. If the Taliban is to be deprived of sanctuary, the Pakistani military would have to change policy. To date, the military leadership and ISI have shown little willingness to withdraw support, and Pakistan's security agencies have been unwilling to apprehend most Afghan Taliban operatives residing in Baluchistan and Karachi. Repeated efforts by the Bush and Obama administrations employing a mix of sticks and carrots have failed to change Pakistan's behavior.

Recommendations for U.S. Policy

Although the American public has grown disillusioned with the U.S. commitment to Afghanistan, the United States retains important interests in targeting terrorist groups that threaten the United States and helping the Afghan government provide for its own security. Much as some would like to disengage as quickly as possible, it is important that the United States continue to help Afghanistan overcome the challenges it faces so that it does not pose a threat to U.S. national interests. Accordingly, the United States should pursue the following recommendations.

PROMOTE MULTIETHNIC COALITIONS FOR THE 2014 ELECTION

U.S. policy should focus on encouraging the formation of multiethnic presidential campaigns—and appointing a representative cabinet for the eventual winner—rather than on backing specific candidates. Prospects for security will improve if the next president and his team receive support, however grudging, from the broad range of political and ethnic groups in Afghanistan.

In practical terms, the White House, State Department, and Defense Department should develop a communications strategy—including synchronizing talking points—that encourages Afghans to achieve political consensus among their most important constituencies. Several Pashtun presidential candidates have already courted ethnic minority running mates to demonstrate inclusivity and secure the support of minority constituencies, but candidates can change their running mates until the election. U.S. officials should reinforce with their Afghan counterparts—in both public comments and private meetings—that

U.S. military and financial support could be severely affected by a fail-ure to reach a consensus on the next president and his team. This mes-sage is important for U.S. officials to repeatedly deliver to presidential candidates, their campaign staffs, and influential powerbrokers.

In their initial meetings after the 2014 election, U.S. officials should encourage the new president to ensure multiethnic representation in the new cabinet, including in such power ministries as the Ministry of Defense, the Ministry of Interior, and the National Directorate of Security. It is particularly important for the new president to secure buy-in from Afghan government officials who control substate militias and ensure that they do not divert resources from state institutions. In addition, U.S. policymakers should publicly and privately reiterate that America's willingness to support the Afghan government financially, diplomatically, and militarily after 2014 will require President Karzai to step down and Afghans to hold a relatively free-and-fair election.[41]

The United States should also help the ANSF secure election sites for the 2014 presidential election. U.S. support from fixed-wing air-craft, helicopters, and unmanned aerial vehicles would aid the ANSF in securing polling stations before—and during—the voting. U.S. officials should also encourage the Pakistan military to deploy additional forces to its border with Afghanistan to diminish insurgent infiltration leading up to the election.

To help reduce the possibility of ballot stuffing, U.S. policymakers should support additional poll-worker screening, expand observer mis-sions at voting centers, and encourage the Afghan government to move the vote-counting process from voting centers to provincial offices. Afghanistan's Independent Election Commission (IEC) is register-ing voters using the same flawed system it used for the 2009 elections. According to some Western diplomats, roughly five million of the sev-enteen million entries in the system may be fraudulent or duplicated. Most entries lack geographic information that would allow IEC offi-cials to help voters identify specific voting stations.[42] The flawed voter registry will almost certainly impede the efforts of the IEC to estimate how many ballots to distribute to voting centers, increasing opportuni-ties for fraud.

ESTABLISH A FOREIGN
INTERNAL DEFENSE MISSION

The United States should pursue a heavy foreign internal defense mission, as defined in U.S. military doctrine, that initially includes between eight thousand and twelve thousand residual American forces. Their mission should be to conduct strikes against terrorists and to train, advise, and assist Afghan national and local forces.[43] U.S. forces would be expected to improve the quality of Afghan forces so that they could establish security in much of Afghanistan and prevent the Taliban from overthrowing the Afghan government.

Maintaining a U.S. military presence in Afghanistan will require U.S. and Afghan governments to conclude a bilateral security agreement. In the meantime, U.S. policymakers should publicly acknowledge their desire to provide an enduring military presence in Afghanistan after 2014. Silence about a U.S. military presence after 2014 will add significant uncertainty to the security situation in Afghanistan. The force package should include a substantial U.S. and NATO special operations component, a reduced number of U.S. and NATO conventional ground and air forces, and CIA paramilitary and other intelligence units to help Afghan forces conduct counterinsurgency and counter-terrorist operations. Several types of U.S. forces would be required to perform these tasks.

Two squadrons of "Tier 1" or other special operations task force units from Joint Special Operations Command would be required to work with Afghan partner units and kill or capture high-value targets. It would also be helpful to draw on allied units, such as British Special Air Service forces. A battalion-sized task force from the 160th Special Operations Aviation Regiment would be useful to provide attack, assault, transport, and reconnaissance missions for the task forces. In addition, approximately three U.S. Army Special Forces battalions and other elements—such as Marine Special Operations Teams and U.S. Navy SEALS—would be necessary to train, advise, and assist Afghan national and local forces. Specific attention should be devoted to addressing the ANSF's weaknesses in such areas as intelligence collection and logistics. This arrangement could include a special operations task force in the east, another in the south, and a third that covers the west and north. Of particular importance would be working with high-end Afghan forces, such as the Afghan National Army Special Forces and Commandos, which are capable of conducting remote-area missions in rural parts of Afghanistan (including Taliban-controlled areas).[44]

Several "enablers" are essential. First, it will be important to retain unmanned aerial vehicles—such as Predators and Reapers—to conduct intelligence, surveillance, reconnaissance, and occasional strike missions. Second, an AC-130 gunship squadron, as well as medical evacuation capabilities, would be required for air support. Third, a brigade-sized conventional force component would be needed to serve as a quick reaction force and to provide security for U.S. bases. Fourth, a battalion-sized conventional unit of security force assistance teams should remain as advisers and liaisons to Afghan security forces, particularly the Afghan National Army. They should be attached at the brigade and corps levels of the Afghan army. It would be helpful to supplement these teams with a comparably sized deployment of NATO security force assistance teams. Fifth, two squadrons of attack aircraft, such as F-15s and A-10s, will be necessary to conduct strikes, depending on desired effects. Other NATO aircraft might also be made available to support this mission. Sixth, some intelligence personnel will need to collect and analyze human and signals intelligence.[45]

A force of eight thousand to twelve thousand troops would cost between $4.7 billion and $7.1 billion per year. These costs would be significantly less than the $113 billion the United States spent in fiscal year 2011 when ninety-eight thousand troops, on average, were deployed to Afghanistan.[46] Some have argued that Afghan force levels should be cut starting in 2015. The United States should continue to support—and help pay for—the current force of 352,000 ANSF, along with 30,000 Afghan Local Police.[47] The Obama administration should make a commitment to provide support to Afghan forces for several years. The administration should refrain from announcing a specific departure date, since the presence of U.S. forces should be determined by the achievement of U.S. objectives like targeting al-Qaeda and ensuring Afghan forces can provide for their own security.

But U.S. military support should not be open-ended. It should be conditions-based rather than calendar-based. The United States should continue military support so long as the United States and Afghanistan reach a bilateral security agreement and the Afghan government follows through on several promises (such as holding a presidential election in 2014). The United States should also continue to assess the state of al-Qaeda and associated terrorist groups.

ENCOURAGE A REALISTIC PEACE PROCESS

U.S. policymakers should conclude that a peace settlement between the Afghan government and the Taliban is unlikely in the foreseeable future for several reasons. First, there is little evidence that the Taliban is serious about a peace settlement at the moment, in part because Taliban leaders appear to believe their prospects for military victory may improve after the U.S. drawdown. Second, few of the conditions that have contributed to peace settlements in past insurgencies exist today in Afghanistan. Outside countries continue to provide support to insurgents, and most Taliban leaders do not view the war as a stalemate. Though a negotiated settlement would be preferable, its prospects appear dim at the moment.

Still, U.S. diplomats should encourage discussions involving the Afghan government (including representatives of the High Peace Council), the Taliban, and regional powers like Pakistan on prisoner exchanges, local cease-fires, and the reintegration of combatants. To date, the most successful discussions between the Afghan government and Taliban representatives have taken place at the local level, not the national level, where both sides have handed over prisoners and established temporary cease-fires. To improve the prospects of a settlement, the United States should support the appointment of a third-party mediator to peace negotiations, such as a representative appointed by the United Nations or from a Persian Gulf country. Third parties have been pivotal in past settlements. In cases where a third-party assisted with implementation of an agreement since World War II, negotiations almost always succeeded, regardless of the initial goals, ideology, or ethnicity of the participants. But if a third party did not help with the implementation of the peace terms, talks almost always failed.[48]

FOCUS ASSISTANCE ON EDUCATION, PUBLIC HEALTH, AND MAINTAINING CURRENT INFRASTRUCTURE

The United States needs to carefully target its civilian assistance dollars. The United States and other donors should provide assistance of $3.3 billion to $3.9 billion a year through 2017, as suggested by the World Bank at the Tokyo Conference, if Afghanistan's government adheres to its commitments under that agreement. If Afghanistan's government does not follow through on its side of the bargain, donors should make graduated reductions in assistances. Assistance is important not only for humanitarian reasons; it is also a crucial investment in the human capital necessary for the long-term development of Afghanistan. As agriculture will remain the most important source of income for the majority of Afghans, the U.S. Agency for International Development should continue to support successful programs in agricultural development.

Over the last decade, investments in Afghanistan's infrastructure, especially roads, have been an important contributor to the rapid increases in GDP and improvements in standards of living Afghanistan has enjoyed. In a period of constrained assistance, Afghanistan's government and donors should focus on setting up and financing effective institutions and policies to maintain this infrastructure. Many countries, including Afghanistan, use taxes on diesel, gasoline, and motor vehicles to finance road construction and repair. Owners and operators of cars and trucks have the financial wherewithal to pay these taxes and are the ones who benefit from the roads. The United States should work with other donors and the government of Afghanistan to improve the collection of motor vehicle taxes and Afghan government funding and oversight of road maintenance.

SUPPORT REGIONAL ECONOMIC INITIATIVES

The United States should support small-scale economic initiatives as a first step to improving relations among countries in the region. U.S. diplomats should support the TAPI pipeline and back financing for the project from multilateral development banks if Turkmenistan, Afghanistan, Pakistan, and India can come to an agreement on right-of-way, financing, pricing, and payments. U.S. diplomats should also support economic détente between Pakistan and India, encouraging Pakistan to follow through on its 2011 decision to grant India most-favored-nation trading status. The United States should encourage India and Pakistan to ease visa restrictions and open more border crossings.

Pakistan presents a particular challenge for the United States because of its support to Afghan insurgent groups. A radical shift of priorities remains unlikely in the near future. The United States, therefore, should take steps to reduce its dependence on Pakistan. The U.S. military should transport as many of its supplies as feasible through the northern route traversing Central Asia, rather than through Pakistan, to hedge against a repetition of the seven-month border closure after the mistaken killing of Pakistani soldiers by NATO forces in November 2011. The United States should also encourage the ISI and Pakistan military to stop providing sanctuary to the Taliban and other militant groups. Specifically, U.S. policymakers should calibrate military assistance to Pakistan in accordance with how much Pakistan confronts—or fails to combat—militant groups like the Taliban, Haqqani network, and Lashkar-e-Taiba. U.S. military aid to Pakistan has already declined from $1.2 billion in 2010 to $849 million in 2012, and should be reduced unless Pakistan curbs its assistance to militant groups.[49] Cuts to military aid should be partially offset by increases in civilian aid, as outlined in the Enhanced Partnership with Pakistan Act of 2009 (the "Kerry-Lugar-Berman" Act). This would avoid repeating the shortsighted abandonment of the 1990s, while directing funds toward the Pakistan people rather than a frequently uncooperative Pakistan military.

The United States has expended an enormous amount of blood and treasure in Afghanistan since 9/11. Though not readily apparent to an American public weary of more than a decade of fighting, important gains have nevertheless been achieved to make Afghanistan a better place. The risk that Afghanistan will once again become a sanctuary for terrorists bent on attacking the United States has been reduced. Yet these gains are reversible. If the recommendations in this report are implemented, Afghanistan will likely be able to contain the insurgency; build upon the the gains in income, education, and health care that have occurred over the past decade; and prevent the reemergence of al-Qaeda and its allies that threaten the United States.

Endnotes

1. Author interviews with Pakistan officials, Washington, September 2013.
2. Jennifer De Pinto, "Public's Views of Afghanistan War Have Turned Sour," *CBS News*, October 5, 2009.
3. Karen DeYoung and Scott Clement, "Many Americans Say Afghan War Isn't Worth Fighting," *Washington Post*, July 25, 2013.
4. Joint Press Conference by President Obama and President Karzai (Washington, DC: The White House, Office of the Press Secretary, January 11, 2013). Also see Joint Statement by President Obama and President Karzai (Washington, DC: The White House, Office of the Press Secretary, January 11, 2013).
5. Remarks by President Obama in Address to the Nation from Afghanistan (Bagram Air Base, Afghanistan: The White House, Office of the Press Secretary, May 1, 2012); Testimony of Ambassador James F. Dobbins, Special Representative for Afghanistan and Pakistan, before the Senate Foreign Relations Committee, July 11, 2013; Testimony of Dr. Peter R. Lavoy, Acting Assistant Secretary of Defense for Asian and Pacific Security Affairs, before the Senate Foreign Relations Committee, July 11, 2013.
6. Vice President Joseph Biden has been among the most optimistic about accomplishing U.S. objectives. In 2012, for instance, he argued: "The fact is, we went [to Afghanistan] for one reason: to get those people who killed Americans, al-Qaeda. We've decimated al-Qaeda central. We have eliminated Osama bin Laden. That was our purpose." See Vice Presidential Debate Transcript, ABC News, October 12, 2012. President Obama similarly noted: "With the devastating blows we've struck against al-Qaeda, our core objective—the reason we went to war in the first place—is now within reach." Joint Press Conference by President Obama and President Karzai (Washington, DC: The White House, Office of the Press Secretary, January 11, 2013).
7. Author interviews with senior U.S. military and intelligence officials, Afghanistan, September 2013.
8. The World Bank, World Development Indicators Dataset, accessed on September 24, 2013.
9. See, for example, Michael O'Hanlon, "The Other Afghan Transition," *Survival* vol. 54, no. 5, October/November 2012, pp. 101–09.
10. Three-quarters of Afghans believe the central government is carrying out its responsibility and is doing a "very good" or a "somewhat good" job. See *Afghanistan in 2012: A Survey of the Afghan People* (San Francisco: The Asia Foundation, 2012), pp. 84–85.
11. Author interview with Western government officials, Afghanistan, June 2013.
12. International Monetary Fund, "Islamic Republic of Afghanistan," Country Report no. 12/245, August 2012.
13. Richard Hogg, Claudia Nassif, Camilo Gomez Osorio, William Byrd, and Andrew Beath, *Afghanistan in Transition: Looking Beyond 2014* (Washington: World Bank, 2013), p. 2.

14. Marc Grossman, "Seven Cities and Two Years: The Diplomatic Campaign in Afghanistan and Pakistan," *Yale Journal of International Affairs*, Summer 2013, pp. 65–75.

15. William Dalrymple, *Return of a King: The Battle for Afghanistan, 1839–42* (New York: Alfred A. Knopf, 2013); Diana Preston, *The Dark Defile: Britain's Catastrophic Invasion of Afghanistan 1838–1842* (New York: Walker & Company, 2012); Steve Coll, *Ghost Wars: The Secret History of the CIA, Afghanistan, and Bin Laden, from the Soviet Invasion to September 10, 2001* (New York: Penguin Press, 2004); Barnett R. Rubin, *The Fragmentation of Afghanistan: State Formation and Collapse in the International System* (New Haven, CT: Yale University Press, 1995).

16. Grossman, "Seven Cities and Two Years: The Diplomatic Campaign in Afghanistan and Pakistan," pp. 65–75.

17. See, for example, U.S. Department of State cable, "Discussing Afghan Policy With the Pakistanis," December 22, 1995; U.S. Embassy (Islamabad) cable, "Afghanistan and Sectarian Violence Contribute to a Souring of Pakistan's Relations With Iran," March 13, 1997. Released by the National Security Archive.

18. In interviews in Afghanistan, several Afghan officials and analysts from Afghan (and Western) nongovernmental organizations argued that a "hands-on" policy by the United States (or other outside states) would undermine the credibility of the 2014 election. Author interviews with Afghan officials and analysts, Afghanistan, September 2013.

19. Michael W. Doyle and Nicholas Sambanis, *Making War and Building Peace* (Princeton, NJ: Princeton University Press, 2006); James Dobbins, et al., *Overcoming Obstacles to Peace: Local Factors in Nation-Building* (Santa Monica, CA: RAND, 2013).

20. General John R. Allen, Michele Flournoy, and Michael O'Hanlon, *Toward a Successful Outcome in Afghanistan* (Washington, DC: Center for a New American Security, May 2013), p. 9.

21. Transparency International, *Corruption Perceptions Index 2012* (Berlin: Transparency International, 2012); World Bank, *Worldwide Governance Indicators* (Washington: World Bank, 2012).

22. On peace settlements see Monica Duffy Toft, *Securing the Peace: The Durable Settlement of Civil Wars* (Princeton, NJ: Princeton University Press, 2009); Virginia Page Fortna, *Peace Time: Cease-Fire Agreements and the Durability of Peace* (Princeton, NJ: Princeton University Press, 2004); Barbara F. Walter, *Committing to Peace: The Successful Settlement of Civil Wars* (Princeton, NJ: Princeton University Press, 2001).

23. See the description of Richard Holbrooke and his team's peace settlement efforts in Vali Nasr, *The Dispensable Nation: American Foreign Policy in Retreat* (New York: Doubleday, 2013).

24. James Shinn and James Dobbins, *Afghan Peace Talks: A Primer* (Santa Monica, CA: RAND, 2011), p. ix.

25. James D. Fearon, "Iraq's Civil War," *Foreign Affairs* vol. 86, no. 2, March/April 2007, p. 8.

26. Monica Duffy Toft, *Securing the Peace: The Durable Settlement of Civil Wars*.

27. Ronald E. Neumann, "Haste Makes Waste," *Foreign Affairs* vol. 91, no. 6, November/December 2012, pp. 167–69.

28. Michael E. O'Hanlon, "A Negotiated Solution for Afghanistan?" *Wall Street Journal*, June 22, 2010; Khalid Mafton, "The Folly of Reconciliation in Afghanistan," *Foreign Policy*, August 29, 2012.

29. The authors considered other options, including options that would involve more than twelve thousand U.S. forces. However, the authors believe a larger number of U.S. troops would be unnecessary to achieve U.S. objectives; a larger number of troops would also probably be politically infeasible.

30. On the "zero option," see Mark Mazzetti and Matthew Rosenberg, "U.S. Considers Faster Pullout in Afghanistan," *New York Times*, July 8, 2013. On broader arguments about withdrawal see, for example, Leslie H. Gelb, "Obama's Faster, Smarter Afghan Exit," *The Daily Beast*, February 1, 2012; Rory Stewart and Gerald Knaus, *Can Intervention Work?* (New York: W.W. Norton, 2011); Stewart, "Trying to Do the Impossible," *Foreign Policy*, March/April 2013, p. 58; Stephen M. Walt, "Don't Prolong the Inevitable," *Foreign Policy*, April 3, 2012.

31. Stewart and Knaus, *Can Intervention Work?*; Stewart, "Trying to Do the Impossible," *Foreign Policy*, March/April 2013, p. 58; Walt, "Don't Prolong the Inevitable"; Walt, "The Real Reason the U.S. Failed in Afghanistan," *Foreign Policy*, March 15, 2013; Richard N. Haass, "The Irony of American Strategy," *Foreign Affairs* vol. 92, no. 3, May/June 2013, pp. 57–67.

32. Gelb, "Obama's Faster, Smarter Afghan Exit."

33. Steven Simon and Jonathan Stevenson, "Afghanistan: How Much Is Enough?" *Survival* vol. 51, no. 5, October/November 2009, pp. 47–67; Paul Pillar, "Is Afghanistan the Right War? No," *The National Interest*, March/April 2010, pp. 33–36.

34. Robert D. Blackwill, "Plan B in Afghanistan," *Foreign Affairs* vol. 90, no. 1, January/February 2011, pp. 42–50.

35. "Foreign internal defense" refers to efforts by the United States to support a host nation's internal defense and development. See *Foreign Internal Defense, Joint Publication 3-22* (Washington, DC: U.S. Department of Defense, July 12, 2010).

36. Milton Bearden, "Curse of the Khyber Pass," *The National Interest*, March/April 2009, pp. 4–12.

37. Author calculations based on average cost per service member from Amy Belasco, "The Cost of Iraq, Afghanistan, and Other Global War on Terror Operations Since 9/11," Congressional Research Service, March 29, 2011, p. 23. Annual operational costs per troop from FY2005 to FY2010 were converted into 2012 dollars using the U.S. GDP deflator and then averaged. The average annual cost, $590,000 in 2012 dollars, was then multiplied by the numbers to be deployed in the scenario. The standard deviation of the time series of the cost per troop was $79,145 in 2012 dollars. Costs do not appear to benefit from economies of scale. Average costs have been lower in periods when the United States has had fewer troops in Afghanistan.

38. Hogg, et al., *Afghanistan in Transition: Looking Beyond 2014*.

39. Sebastian Abbot, "Sharif's Win Sparks Hope for Pakistan-India Ties," *Associated Press*, May 15, 2013.

40. Seth G. Jones, *Counterinsurgency in Afghanistan* (Santa Monica, CA: RAND, 2008).

41. See, for example, O'Hanlon, "The Other Afghan Transition," pp. 101–09.

42. Author interviews with Western government officials, Afghanistan, June 2013.

43. "Local forces" refer to tribal, subtribal, and other substate forces that exist in Afghanistan.

44. These U.S. special operations forces could also conduct what is called "unconventional warfare" in U.S. Army doctrine and work by, with, or through irregular forces in Afghanistan against the Taliban. U.S. Department of the Army, *Army Special Operations Forces Unconventional Warfare* (Washington, DC: Headquarters, Department of the Army, September 2008).

45. On force packages see, for example, Austin Long, "Small Is Beautiful: The Counterterrorism Option in Afghanistan," *Orbis* vol. 54, no. 2, Spring 2010, pp. 199–214; LTG David W. Barno (ret.) and Andrew Exum, *Responsible Transition: Securing U.S. Interests in Afghanistan Beyond 2011* (Washington, DC: Center for a New American Security, December 2010).

46. Office of the Secretary of Defense Comptroller as cited in Anthony Cordesman, "The U.S. Cost of the Afghan War: FY2002–FY2013," Center for Strategic and International Studies, Washington, D.C., May 14, 2012, p. 7.

47. See, for example, Frederick W. Kagan, "The Afghan Endgame," *Weekly Standard*, February 25, 2013.

48. Walter, *Committing to Peace: The Successful Settlement of Civil Wars*.

49. U.S. military assistance includes 1206 funding; counternarcotics funds; foreign military financing; international military education and training; international narcotics control and law enforcement; nonproliferation, antiterrorism, demining, and related; and Pakistan counterinsurgency fund/Pakistan counterinsurgency capability fund. See, for example, Susan B. Epstein and K. Alan Kronstadt, *Pakistan: U.S. Foreign Assistance* (Washington, DC: Congressional Research Service, July 2013).

About the Authors

Seth G. Jones is associate director of the International Security and Defense Policy Center at the RAND Corporation, as well as an adjunct professor at Johns Hopkins University's School for Advanced International Studies (SAIS). He served as the representative to the assistant secretary of defense for special operations for the commander, U.S. Special Operations Command. Before that, he served as a plans officer and adviser to the commanding general, U.S. Special Operations Forces, in Afghanistan (Combined Forces Special Operations Component Command–Afghanistan). He is the author of *Hunting in the Shadows: The Pursuit of al Qa'ida after 9/11* and *In the Graveyard of Empires: America's War in Afghanistan*, which won the 2010 Council on Foreign Relations Silver Medal for Best Book of the Year. He is also the author of *The Rise of European Security Cooperation*. Jones has published articles in a range of journals, such as *Foreign Policy* and *International Security*, as well as in newspapers and magazines such as *Foreign Affairs*, the *New York Times*, *Washington Post*, and *Wall Street Journal*, and various RAND publications. He received his AB from Bowdoin College and his MA and PhD from the University of Chicago.

Keith Crane is director of the RAND environment, energy, and economic development program as well as a professor at the Pardee RAND Graduate School. In fall 2003, he served as an economic policy adviser to the Coalition Provisional Authority in Baghdad. Prior to rejoining RAND in February 2002, he was chief operating officer and director of research at PlanEcon, Inc., a research and consulting firm based in Washington, DC, focusing on central and eastern Europe and the former Soviet republics. During his tenure at PlanEcon, Crane provided analysis and economic forecasts used in over one hundred major investments in the region. He writes extensively on transition issues in policy and academic journals, and briefs high-level decision-makers. Crane received his BA from the University of Minnesota and his MA and PhD in economics from Indiana University.

Advisory Committee for
Afghanistan After the Drawdown

Peter Ackerman
Rockport Capital, Inc.

Stephen D. Biddle, *ex officio*
George Washington University

John A. Gastright
DynCorp International

Marc Grossman
The Cohen Group

Frederick W. Kagan
American Enterprise Institute
for Public Policy Research

Clare Lockhart
Institute for State Effectiveness

Steve Mann
Exxon Mobil Corporation

Daniel S. Markey, *ex officio*
Council on Foreign Relations

Paul D. Miller
RAND Corporation

Ronald E. Neumann
American Academy of Diplomacy

David E. Sanger
New York Times

Paul B. Stares, *ex officio*
Council on Foreign Relations

Ashley J. Tellis
Carnegie Endowment for International Peace

Andrew Wilder
U.S. Institute of Peace

Micah Zenko, *ex officio*
Council on Foreign Relations

CPA Advisory Committee

Mission Statement of the
Center for Preventive Action

The Center for Preventive Action (CPA) seeks to help prevent, defuse, or resolve deadly conflicts around the world and to expand the body of knowledge on conflict prevention. It does so by creating a forum in which representatives of governments, international organizations, nongovernmental organizations, corporations, and civil society can gather to develop operational and timely strategies for promoting peace in specific conflict situations. The center focuses on conflicts in countries or regions that affect U.S. interests, but may be otherwise overlooked; where prevention appears possible; and when the resources of the Council on Foreign Relations can make a difference. The center does this by

- Issuing Council Special Reports to evaluate and respond rapidly to developing conflict situations and formulate timely, concrete policy recommendations that the U.S. government and international and local actors can use to limit the potential for deadly violence.

- Engaging the U.S. government and news media in conflict prevention efforts. CPA staff members meet with administration officials and members of Congress to brief on CPA findings and recommendations; facilitate contacts between U.S. officials and important local and external actors; and raise awareness among journalists of potential flashpoints around the globe.

- Building networks with international organizations and institutions to complement and leverage the Council's established influence in the U.S. policy arena and increase the impact of CPA recommendations.

- Providing a source of expertise on conflict prevention to include research, case studies, and lessons learned from past conflicts that policymakers and private citizens can use to prevent or mitigate future deadly conflicts.

Council Special Reports

Published by the Council on Foreign Relations

The Future of U.S. Special Operations Forces
Linda Robinson; CSR No. 66, April 2013

Reforming U.S. Drone Strike Policies
Micah Zenko; CSR No. 65, January 2013
A Center for Preventive Action Report

Countering Criminal Violence in Central America
Michael Shifter; CSR No. 64, April 2012
A Center for Preventive Action Report

Saudi Arabia in the New Middle East
F. Gregory Gause III; CSR No. 63, December 2011
A Center for Preventive Action Report

Partners in Preventive Action: The United States and International Institutions
Paul B. Stares and Micah Zenko; CSR No. 62, September 2011
A Center for Preventive Action Report

Justice Beyond The Hague: Supporting the Prosecution of International Crimes in National Courts
David A. Kaye; CSR No. 61, June 2011

The Drug War in Mexico: Confronting a Shared Threat
David A. Shirk; CSR No. 60, March 2011
A Center for Preventive Action Report

UN Security Council Enlargement and U.S. Interests
Kara C. McDonald and Stewart M. Patrick; CSR No. 59, December 2010
An International Institutions and Global Governance Program Report

Congress and National Security
Kay King; CSR No. 58, November 2010

Toward Deeper Reductions in U.S. and Russian Nuclear Weapons
Micah Zenko; CSR No. 57, November 2010
A Center for Preventive Action Report

Internet Governance in an Age of Cyber Insecurity
Robert K. Knake; CSR No. 56, September 2010
An International Institutions and Global Governance Program Report

Averting Crisis in Ukraine
Steven Pifer; CSR No. 41, January 2009
A Center for Preventive Action Report

Congo: Securing Peace, Sustaining Progress
Anthony W. Gambino; CSR No. 40, October 2008
A Center for Preventive Action Report

Deterring State Sponsorship of Nuclear Terrorism
Michael A. Levi; CSR No. 39, September 2008

China, Space Weapons, and U.S. Security
Bruce W. MacDonald; CSR No. 38, September 2008

Sovereign Wealth and Sovereign Power: The Strategic Consequences of American Indebtedness
Brad W. Setser; CSR No. 37, September 2008
A Maurice R. Greenberg Center for Geoeconomic Studies Report

Securing Pakistan's Tribal Belt
Daniel S. Markey; CSR No. 36, July 2008 (Web-only release) and August 2008
A Center for Preventive Action Report

Avoiding Transfers to Torture
Ashley S. Deeks; CSR No. 35, June 2008

Global FDI Policy: Correcting a Protectionist Drift
David M. Marchick and Matthew J. Slaughter; CSR No. 34, June 2008
A Maurice R. Greenberg Center for Geoeconomic Studies Report

Dealing with Damascus: Seeking a Greater Return on U.S.-Syria Relations
Mona Yacoubian and Scott Lasensky; CSR No. 33, June 2008
A Center for Preventive Action Report

Climate Change and National Security: An Agenda for Action
Joshua W. Busby; CSR No. 32, November 2007
A Maurice R. Greenberg Center for Geoeconomic Studies Report

Planning for Post-Mugabe Zimbabwe
Michelle D. Gavin; CSR No. 31, October 2007
A Center for Preventive Action Report

The Case for Wage Insurance
Robert J. LaLonde; CSR No. 30, September 2007
A Maurice R. Greenberg Center for Geoeconomic Studies Report

Reform of the International Monetary Fund
Peter B. Kenen; CSR No. 29, May 2007
A Maurice R. Greenberg Center for Geoeconomic Studies Report

Nuclear Energy: Balancing Benefits and Risks
Charles D. Ferguson; CSR No. 28, April 2007

Nigeria: Elections and Continuing Challenges
Robert I. Rotberg; CSR No. 27, April 2007
A Center for Preventive Action Report

The Economic Logic of Illegal Immigration
Gordon H. Hanson; CSR No. 26, April 2007
A Maurice R. Greenberg Center for Geoeconomic Studies Report

The United States and the WTO Dispute Settlement System
Robert Z. Lawrence; CSR No. 25, March 2007
A Maurice R. Greenberg Center for Geoeconomic Studies Report

Bolivia on the Brink
Eduardo A. Gamarra; CSR No. 24, February 2007
A Center for Preventive Action Report

After the Surge: The Case for U.S. Military Disengagement From Iraq
Steven N. Simon; CSR No. 23, February 2007

Darfur and Beyond: What Is Needed to Prevent Mass Atrocities
Lee Feinstein; CSR No. 22, January 2007

Avoiding Conflict in the Horn of Africa: U.S. Policy Toward Ethiopia and Eritrea
Terrence Lyons; CSR No. 21, December 2006
A Center for Preventive Action Report

Living with Hugo: U.S. Policy Toward Hugo Chávez's Venezuela
Richard Lapper; CSR No. 20, November 2006
A Center for Preventive Action Report

Reforming U.S. Patent Policy: Getting the Incentives Right
Keith E. Maskus; CSR No. 19, November 2006
A Maurice R. Greenberg Center for Geoeconomic Studies Report

Foreign Investment and National Security: Getting the Balance Right
Alan P. Larson and David M. Marchick; CSR No. 18, July 2006
A Maurice R. Greenberg Center for Geoeconomic Studies Report

Challenges for a Postelection Mexico: Issues for U.S. Policy
Pamela K. Starr; CSR No. 17, June 2006 (web-only release) and November 2006

U.S.-India Nuclear Cooperation: A Strategy for Moving Forward
Michael A. Levi and Charles D. Ferguson; CSR No. 16, June 2006

Generating Momentum for a New Era in U.S.-Turkey Relations
Steven A. Cook and Elizabeth Sherwood-Randall; CSR No. 15, June 2006

Peace in Papua: Widening a Window of Opportunity
Blair A. King; CSR No. 14, March 2006
A Center for Preventive Action Report

Neglected Defense: Mobilizing the Private Sector to Support Homeland Security
Stephen E. Flynn and Daniel B. Prieto; CSR No. 13, March 2006

Afghanistan's Uncertain Transition From Turmoil to Normalcy
Barnett R. Rubin; CSR No. 12, March 2006
A Center for Preventive Action Report

Preventing Catastrophic Nuclear Terrorism
Charles D. Ferguson; CSR No. 11, March 2006

Getting Serious About the Twin Deficits
Menzie D. Chinn; CSR No. 10, September 2005
A Maurice R. Greenberg Center for Geoeconomic Studies Report

Both Sides of the Aisle: A Call for Bipartisan Foreign Policy
Nancy E. Roman; CSR No. 9, September 2005

Forgotten Intervention? What the United States Needs to Do in the Western Balkans
Amelia Branczik and William L. Nash; CSR No. 8, June 2005
A Center for Preventive Action Report

A New Beginning: Strategies for a More Fruitful Dialogue with the Muslim World
Craig Charney and Nicole Yakatan; CSR No. 7, May 2005

Power-Sharing in Iraq
David L. Phillips; CSR No. 6, April 2005
A Center for Preventive Action Report

*Giving Meaning to "Never Again": Seeking an Effective Response to the Crisis
in Darfur and Beyond*
Cheryl O. Igiri and Princeton N. Lyman; CSR No. 5, September 2004

Freedom, Prosperity, and Security: The G8 Partnership with Africa: Sea Island 2004 and Beyond
J. Brian Atwood, Robert S. Browne, and Princeton N. Lyman; CSR No. 4, May 2004

Addressing the HIV/AIDS Pandemic: A U.S. Global AIDS Strategy for the Long Term
Daniel M. Fox and Princeton N. Lyman; CSR No. 3, May 2004
Cosponsored with the Milbank Memorial Fund

Challenges for a Post-Election Philippines
Catharin E. Dalpino; CSR No. 2, May 2004
A Center for Preventive Action Report

Stability, Security, and Sovereignty in the Republic of Georgia
David L. Phillips; CSR No. 1, January 2004
A Center for Preventive Action Report

Note: Council Special Reports are available for download from CFR's website, www.cfr.org.
For more information, email publications@cfr.org.